Rag & Bone

Poems by
Kathryn Nuernberger

Author Photo: Brian Blair

Cover Photos: Brian Blair

Book Design: Joel A. Bass

ISBN: 978-1-932418-40-8

Elixir Press
PO Box 27029
Denver, Colorado 80227

www.ElixirPress.com

Library of Congress Cataloging-in-Publication Data

Nuernberger, Kathryn.
Rag & bone : poems / by Kathryn Nuernberger.
p. cm.
Winner of the 2010 Antivenom Poetry Award.
ISBN 978-1-932418-40-8 (alk. paper)
I. Title. II. Title: Rag and bone.
PS3614.U43R34 2011
811'.6--dc22

2011000284

Elixir Press is a nonprofit literary organization.

Rag & Bone

Poems by
Kathryn Nuernberger

for Jim —
Thanks for hosting us
at the stabbin' cabin.
There's nowhere I'd rather be.

Kate

Elixir Press

Contents

Introduction

Reflecting on the source of poetry, Yeats recalled a "mound of refuse or the sweepings of a street,/Old kettles, old bottles, and a broken can,/Old iron, old bones, old rags"—the storied refuse of human lives, battered testaments of loss that, through art, were ultimately rescued. *Rag & Bone,* Kathryn Nuernberger's compelling debut collection, recalls this transformative vision, taking for its presiding genius the rag and bone man, a near-mythological figure who walks "the ornate bridges of your city/picking up junk from the bins behind/the flea market, reciting to himself/old poems children don't read anymore."

Whatever the dangers of hoarding (the rag man's "coin collection/ alone would drag his vessel to the bottom/of the sea"), Nuernberger refuses to "abandon a ruined thing"; it is the poet's sacred duty to remember and restore. In salvage lie magic and mystery: things that go missing may be found, all that's lost one day "resurrected from rust." With chiseled beauty and measured grace, *Rag & Bone* forms a fiercely intelligent meditation on the power of our gaze and the perils within it.

Nuernberger is drawn to spectrums both visible and invisible, to what appears to and to what eludes the eye: koi fish fed bread crumbs in a Botanical Garden's pond introduce children to the natural world's beauties and dangers; anatomical skeletons in the classroom shed light on our shared metaphysical fate. The fecundity of backyard gardens recalls the rich kingdom of fairy tale and fable, no less strange or further off than the present moment.

"How hard it is to see clearly," Nuernberger observes. "Translations," the poet's musings on the nature of color, form a powerful counterpoint to her meditation on language and experience. "When I look out the window and say green," she says,

> . . . I mean sea-green
> I mean moss green, I mean gray, I mean pale and also
> electrically flecked with white and I mean green
> in its damp way of glowing off a leaf.

Newly pregnant, this speaker is pleased to learn the Greek term for the color she sees. *Chlorol*, study teaches her, is "one of the untranslatable words," a term that shifts her understanding of the visible world that she expects to show her child. When that child is lost in a miscarriage, she struggles to find apt words to frame the grief in whose aftermath the pregnancy itself appears as a cruel trompe l'oeil, a mere trick of light: it is "as if the baby had fallen away/like a blue shadow on the snow."

Elsewhere, Nuernberger probes the motives and effects of human inquiry. In "The Ragged Edge," the book's opening poem, her reflections take shape against the backdrop of cognitive studies. A grisly brain experiment on lab monkeys and a primatologist's video of chimps "swinging in ritualized arcs/over a great waterfall" (said to reveal "'the dawn of awe and wonder'") show the poet something else altogether: civilizations's many contradictions, embodied in the "severed head" of the monkey "knitted to a ragged neck." The image, documented for posterity in strict black and white—empirical evidence of scientific success—holds a viewer in thrall. According to the poet, "You can't help but recoil." For Nuernberger, looking is an aesthetic choice with moral ramifications as well as implicit disappointment, an act "not unlike staring at pornography—/what you see is never quite what you wanted."

Throughout *Rag & Bone*, Nuernberger returns to the question of what we want and what we'll do to get it—in private and in public. "U.S. EPA Reg. No. 524-474" reflects on the "surgical" ease of bio-engineering:

> . . . Have you seen what can be
> done with tobacco and fireflies?
> Just for the hell of it, whole Virginian fields
> now glow under the passing planes.
> Salmon-tomatoes clutch their fishy gloss against
> the pinch of frost. I think I'll give it a try.

And try the speaker does, taking the ".22 shell/dipped in DNA solution at the stem" a loved one gave her to help her "feel better." Power invites, excites, transforms: "peppermint termites" "sweeten the swarm," rats can be "larynxed" with "mockingbird tales." But repair fractures between lovers? Nuernberger's speaker knows better than to bet on it. Having "made a bullet of me to blast/into your amber eye," she says,

> . . . you could arch each disaffected synapse
> without noticing me careening through
> about to hybridize the brick at the other side
> of your exit wound. . .

This is a poetry of pain and power, a language of grief and cautious hope; for Nuernberger, "Luck is a mean-hoofed beast" that "likes to catch you by surprise." When Luck visits, we must not name what we love "or he will think you've grown attached." Yet memory survives, whatever ill luck befalls our loved ones, as we find in Nuernberger's elegy to her solitary grandfather: "though I too/am a sophisticate/who scorns musicals,/I was once a little girl/who stood in my grand-/father's living room/singing, *Cuckoo!/Cuckoo!* While he sipped/his scotch and laughed/at my preciosity."

Whether describing the precise coloration of fruit skin, the contours of memory, or secrets of Fatima which turn out to be "cryptic mumbo jumbo," *Rag & Bone* reveals complicated truths with rare eloquence and wit. Whatever the future holds, Nuernberger remembers, even as she beholds the present with blinding intensity. Lyrical and deeply felt, the poems in *Rag & Bone* track the movement of a sometimes skeptical but always engaged and impassioned mind.

Jane Satterfield

For Brian, my first reader and best love.

I.

THE RAGGED EDGE

In 1963 and again in 2001 a scientist attached
a monkey's head to another monkey's body
one blood vessel at a time.

When you get right down to it, the lab assistant
says, nothing could be simpler.

The disembodied brain runs on the machine
of a decapitated trunk, and if you say

the word *awe* doesn't come to mind,
you're a liar.

What was it like? For the monkeys no one can say.
The severed nerves hang loose,
resulting in near total paralysis.

But the mouth could still bite the hand
that tried to adjust a tube running into its flared nostrils.
And it did. Which was evidence of a tremendous success –

one sign of life is the defense
of whatever body you have left.

A primatologist finally caught on video
a family of chimps swinging in ritualized arcs
over a great waterfall.

Her voice wavers in the background as she narrates,
"Apparently lost in contemplation,
the chimpanzee cries out, runs excitedly back and forth
and drums on trees with its fists.

Here we see the dawn of awe and wonder."

Human rituals tend to involve putting things together
or taking them apart.

In church I learned that through sacramental sex
you see the face of God.
Another thing I learned was the body is a vessel
for sin – try to forget you have one.

Once upon a time a severed head
was knitted to a ragged neck and the only
pictures are in black and white.

You can't help but recoil, to use the words *horror*
or *vulgarity*. It's not unlike staring at pornography –
what you see is never quite what you wanted.

The doctor's shadow obscures the stitched line
where you thought you'd see how one became the other.

ICHTHYPHOBIA

Two of the bad girls from the neighborhood got drunk,
climbed the fence into the Botanical Garden
to skinny dip, and drowned.

My brother said the koi pulled them down.
Their funerals were closed casket because of what
the fish did to their faces.

This was at the pond with a zigzag bridge where
my brother gave a push and said not to cry,
to be such a girl.

The zigzag prevents evil spirits from giving chase.
Evil spirits like the kappa, who is the size
of a ten-year-old boy.

Sometimes he sucks the flesh of a girl –
her shoulder, her wrist – a nip. And sometimes
he sucks her whole life

out with heaving breaths. Don't believe? Play a game
of pull-finger with the face swimming in the water
and just see

if he doesn't drag you in. For a quarter we could feed
the koi bread crumbs, which is how they'd grown
to the size of possums.

I threw the pieces quickly and looked away
from the clamor of fleshy pink yawns jostled
by waves and slick bodies,

but still felt the fish set upon my skin, mouths everywhere,
dark water closing in. If the kappa has stolen your daughter,
there is little to do.

But if she is your precious daughter, your only one,
try carving her name into a Yubari melon. The kappa may
make the trade,

or he may keep both fruits. According to Freud,
the child who wishes to join society must repress
the memory of infancy's

unfettered genitals. The kappa never forgot.
When he comes, your only chance is to bow and bow.
He cannot resist your manners,

even though the crown of his head is an indented bowl,
even though he knows it's the clear broth of his brain
spilling into that cold, dark water and its gathering fish.

U.S. EPA REG. NO. 524-474

Gene-splicing the beetle-resistant Basillus
Thuringiensis with a potato sounds surgical,
but it's just a matter of firing a .22 shell
dipped in DNA solution at the stem
straggling out from the russet eye. If you're lucky
the hybrid sticks. Have you seen what can be
done with tobacco and fireflies?
Just for the hell of it, whole Virginian fields
now glow under the passing planes.
Salmon-tomatoes clutch their fishy gloss against
the pinch of frost. I think I'll give it a try.
I have the gun you gave me. You said
I'd feel better if I held it awhile. I feel better,
and I'm not giving it back. I'm firing shrimp
into pigeons and dipping the de-veined crescents
of their wings in cocktail sauce. Thinking of you,
I made peppermint termites to sweeten
the swarm, and larynxed the rats with mockingbird
calls. I shot scorpion tails into the fighting
fish, and now I've made a bullet of me to blast
into your amber eye. Will you come out simpering
like a girl? Eager to perform your vulnerabilities?
Will you recoil at the site of a baited hook? Or will I
pass right through imploding flowers of viscera
without having scratched a rung on your double helix?
I'd wager you could arch each disaffected synapse
without even noticing me careening through
about to hybridize the brick at the other side
of your exit wound. Give a stone a language
chromosome and it'll run with words like water.
It'll announce in spray-painted letters that it hearts
you, that it can't live without you. That it would

rip out its own mortar just to think you might
take a concrete crumb to jingle in your empty pocket
as you remember what I used to be.

IN THE VEGETABLE GARDEN

Fence to fence all is pea vines trellising
up the walls and pumpkins strewn across
the paths. The bountiful grid turned
tangle, so lush a small child could be lost
in the tomatoes, come out stained red
and pulpy a decade later calling me Mom
in a new, deep voice, the same rooty timbre
used by the carrots who raised him.
And I would kiss him all over, remembering
too well how his pale little boy legs dangled
over my arms, already too big to hold.

TRANSLATIONS

I want to believe we can't see anything
we don't have a word for.

When I look out the window and say green, I mean sea green,
I mean moss green, I mean gray, I mean pale and also
electrically flecked with white and I mean green
in its damp way of glowing off a leaf.

Scheele's green, the green of Renaissance painters,
is a sodium carbonate solution heated to ninety degrees
as arsenious oxide is stirred in. Sodium displaces copper,
resulting in a green precipitate that is sometimes used
as insecticide. When I say green I mean
a shiny green bug eating a yellow leaf.

Before synthetics, not every painter could afford a swathe
of blue. Shocking pink, aka neon, aka kinky pink,
wasn't even on the market. I want to believe Andy Warhol
invented it in 1967 and ever since no one's eyes
have been the same. There were sunsets before,
but without that hot shocking neon Marilyn, a desert sky
was just cataract smears. I want to believe this.

The pale green of lichen and half-finished leaves
filling my window is a palette very far from carnation
or bougainvillea, but to look out is to understand it is not,
is to understand what it is not. I stare out the window a lot.
Between the beginning and the end the leaves unfolded.
I looked out one morning and everything was unfamiliar
as if I was looking at the green you could only see
if you'd never known synthetic colors existed.

I've drawn into myself people say.
We understand, they say.

There are people who only have words for red
and black and white, and I wonder if they even see
the trees at the edge of the grass
or the green storms coming out of the west.
There are people who use the same word for green
and red and brown, and I wonder if red
seems so urgently bright pouring from the body
when there is no green for it to fall against.

In his treatise on color Wittgenstein asked,
"Can't we imagine certain people
having a different geometry of colour than we do?"

I want to believe the eye doesn't see green until it has a name,
because I don't want anything to look the way it did before.

Van Gogh painted pink flowers, but the pink faded
and curators labeled the work "White Roses" by mistake.

The world in my window is a color the Greeks called *chlorol*.
When I learned the word I was newly pregnant
and the first pale lichens had just speckled the silver branches.
The pines and the lichens in the chill drizzle were glowing green
and a book in my lap said chlorol was one of the untranslatable
words. The vibrating glow pleased me then, as a finger
dipped in sugar pleased me then. I said the word aloud
for the baby to hear. Chlorol. I imagined the baby
could only see hot pink and crimson inside its tiny universe,
but if you can see what I'm seeing, the word for it
is chlorol. It's one of the things you'll like out here.

Nineteenth century critics mocked painters who cast shadows
in unexpected colors. After noticing green cypresses do drop red
shadows, Goethe chastised them. "The eye demands
completeness and seeks to eke out the colorific circle in itself."
He tells of a trick of light that had him pacing a row of poppies
to see the flaming petals again and figure out why.

Over and over again Wittgenstein frets the problem of translucence.
Why is there no clear white?
He wants to see the world through white-tinted glasses,
but all he finds is mist.

At first I felt as if the baby had fallen away
like a blue shadow on the snow.

Then I felt like I killed the baby
in the way you can be thinking about something else
and drop a heavy platter by mistake.

Sometimes I feel like I was stupid
to have thought I was pregnant at all.

Color is an illusion, a response to the vibrating universe
of electrons. Light strikes a leaf and there's an explosion
where it lands. When colors change, electromagnetic fields
are colliding. The wind is not the only thing moving the trees.

Once when I went into those woods I saw a single hot pink orchid
on the hillside and I had to keep reminding myself not to
tell the baby about the beautiful small things I was seeing.
So, hot pink has been here forever and I don't even care
about that color or how Andy Warhol showed me an orchid.
I hate pink. It makes my eyes burn.

PAUVRE BÊTE

Once in the trees lived a minotaur
who could not understand the language of leaves,

even though he was an illusion made
of their shadowy green. Even though he spoke
to himself in the broken accent of twigs.

When the wind blew the leaves flailed
their arms against his thatched snorting.

When the wind blew he bent over them,
devoured them, and grew. He grew

over the fire escape and down the brush
alleys, gathering into himself the tree-lined
avenues and boulevards. The minotaur grew

until the leaves' mercy, their shushing word
please, was forgotten entirely. Silence
and the beast's creak ragged winds.

He howled for more leaves but he was
the god of them, the body of them.
His broken bellows were unappeasable.

PRIMA DONNA IN HER HEAVEN

For her birthday God's daughter asked
Him for a mechanical golden bird,
but was given a garden under glass.
Here is some life, He said, for you to cherish
and to teach you responsibility.

Life oozed around on its green island,
smelling like vulture's breath and waving
billions of fleshy tentacles at the sky.
The birthday girl thought it was a stupid toy
and she tried never to look at it.

Disappointment was a goat's head hanging
in her stomach. In time politeness passed,
and she put the present out of her room to be
shattered or buried or sold at a tag sale. By then
everyone in the garden had forgotten her face.

A watchmaker steps out into the dawn.
The dome of sky is fogged with dew and in the tree
his nightingale cocks a golden head
with clicking blinks. A tinny aria chirps out
through the plum blossoms, then echoes back.

BESIDE HERSELF

The woman who could not
pay attention fell in love,
but could not remember.
Was it with chipping brick
or was it wrought iron
trellis? And trellis or church
bells or perhaps oxidized copper
pipes was waiting to love her,
waiting through the years
she spent studying
her fingers through closed
eyes thinking only of her
love, her overcast sky,
her devoted cup of tin
coins, darling dearest scarf
with lavender fringe.
She hardly even stopped
to wonder why she could
never hold on. It must
have been the train schedule
she was thinking of,
the way every thought flips away
before she can say departure
or arrival. Or was it the wasp
trapped by the glass? She thinks
she might be disappearing.
Everyone rushing past
is careful not to touch eyes.
Everyone reminds her
of her love, her quartz-
flecked concrete glittering
like a cold breath rising

into the sun, then evaporating
into particles of nitrogen,
oxygen, argon and the rest,
which she can't see to love,
so loves instead their scattered
blue light, a halo fading out
into the vacuum of space.

FOR EMILY, WHO CAME SOMETIMES TO WATCH THE RAIN

We were a pair of lonely frogs.

She was afraid
of other children too,
and we were friends

when I could see her,
which was rare –

frogs are such solitary creatures.

Black crows above us settled on the tree.
The only view: night's wings
endlessly preened. A frog can gulp,
but she cannot scream.

She liked breaks in storm
when light descends like fog
and we are caught

in a strata of sun
compressed by a fist
of ashen clouds, oil-slicked
asphalt shining like stained glass,

when, weary with pale existence,
that sun alights on every leaf.

I should have called them all to see,

but I was not that kind of child,
and she was not that kind of dream.

STILL LIFE

How hard it is to see clearly.

Take this grape. It's violet,
but not quite, magenta,
but not quite.

More the amethyst night
of a lighted bridge
when there's a bit of dawn
and you've been out late,
lying in the park next to
your best friend,
and you've gotten
that rustling feeling out
of your chest for a minute.

Only not quite.

More the color of her coffin
with its deep-wood shine
carried under the stained glass
as the choir sings, but no sound,
as you sing, but no sound.

More the shade of that perfect quiet.

Only not quite so perfectly round,
or perfectly dark, but reflecting
the white light of morning
on its shriveling skin
as one last thing that was hers
passes the plum shadow,

the wrinkled fig, of your pursed lips.

And now where there was fruit,
there are thorns. Not thorns
exactly, but woody fingers,
green tattered ends without name,
more green than yellow, more
green than brown, but not
green, not exactly green.

THE STRANGE GIRL ASKS POLITELY
TO BE CALLED PRINCESS

When the strange girl skips rope her hair flies
like a porpoise. She collects things that melt
and things that tick, circles and cubes
and checkerboards in a drawer

she can pull out from her navel.
Other children, alerted by the rumble
of marbles in her chest, chase her
across the field. She insists she is only

hungry, but they pin her down and open her
up. Cockroaches rush out and bullies run
and squeal, crushing carapaces underfoot.
She gathers as many as she can,

tells them she's sorry there is no lock. She's sorry,
but good children shouldn't have secrets.

PAUL KLEE'S PUPPET THEATER:
MR. DEATH AND ELECTRICAL SPOOK

Mr. Death was a present for Felix at nine.
His plaster face is a rough and gauzy spackle,
but mostly it is the yawn of black-cavern eyes
and etched tread of charcoaled teeth.
Mr. Death wears white burlap like a jazz funeral
and was the only puppet in his box to survive
the bombing, then the fire in 1945.

> *Ich bin der Tod und ess' kein Brot*
> *und trink' kein Bier.*
> *Da hilft kein' Bitt'!*

Felix the boy played a game with the lights
where he turned them off and turned them on
and became happy and delighted.

Electrical Spook came after the war with a fuse
for a head like a periscope that rises up
to look around and blink its big lid.
He also lived in a box and no one
can say if his lightning body, yellow and red,
turned dark when the top was shut.

Also in the box was Klee's self-portrait,
a puppet with extremely large pupils
and a square face carved from a beef bone.

> *I am death and eat no bread*
> *and drink no beer,* Mr. Death used to say.

Electrical Spook would turn the lights off.

You must come with me!
Your pleas are empty, Mr. Death used to say.

Electrical Spook would turn the lights on.

Be willing or I shall use force, Mr. Death used to say,
according to Felix, who is very old by now
or dead by now, but remembers well the games
he played when his father was still around.

Electrical Spook would turn the lights off.

THE CHILDREN'S MUSEUM

These children who are not my children
smear the microscopic scales of a monarch's
black eye across the greenhouse glass.
They pinch each other and laugh
when someone cries. The youngest traces
 a tiger-striped wing and growls. He wants
to be a predator, wants to hear a story.
His mother wants me to keep him happy,
so I tell the one

> where a gnome lived in the forest
> robber-barons devoured to fuel
> their chimneys. Grass turned black
> and bluebirds gray. Dewberries
> tasted like rotten meat and the
> hungry gnome had nowhere to
> go but the city, where a boy he
> knew once had grown into a man.
> But grownups seldom remember
> their childhood friends, least of
> all the ones who appear in winter
> smelling like refugees.

This moral makes the children
angry. They jump up to disagree.
They are the uncorrupted innocents
and they will remember everything.

A NICE GIRL

I was traveling with a man I wanted
to love. It seemed ethical. When we got high
I promised to love him forever. He said
I was the best thing that ever happened.
He'd quit the cocaine but too late
to straighten a deviated septum. After the surgery,
his face was all bruise. If we'd stayed,
the doctor could have told him the skin graft
in his sinus was dying. Instead, we took off
with the painkillers to see some band in Miami.

Three days sleeping in the Coral Court Motel
and I wondered if love was nothing more
than the strength to be kind. He started
by kissing my ear. I smelled something, dead,
maybe in the furnace, or behind the wall.
I couldn't concentrate when everything
was so rank, when the stench got worse
each time he leaned for my mouth.
He was tender and devastated,
sitting naked on the end of the bed. "It's me,"
he said. "It's me who smells rotten."

But he couldn't smell a thing. My cheek
prickled with the small stabs
of loose stitches. He couldn't feel those either.
This was what I deserved
for following him in the first place.
A nice girl would have kissed him,
straddled him on that stained mattress.
She'd never have left him sitting alone
in a white plastic deck chair watching the tide

dump black seaweed on the shore
as he held a rag filled with ice to his face.

GLEEMAN

The tiny man in my chest juggles knives.
It's an impossible situation. His tosses
slide right through my flesh, as if I were
water. I feel every serrated edge, but see –

> *She unbuttons her shirt to show*
> *the penny arcade nestled inside. Drop a quarter*
> *in her palm and the red curtain rises*
> *to reveal a gleeman on the empty stage.*

No blood.

> *The tiny man looks tired. His shirt is wrinkled*
> *and dirty hair hangs over his ears, but he's very good.*
> *He never takes his eyes off the audience. Never even*
> *glances at the blades. Such balance!*

I hate that painted face. And his hair.
I offered to trim it, but...
He pretends he doesn't understand
his appearance reflects on me.

> *What a showman! The knives are circling in orbit,*
> *and still he manages to catch one behind his back,*
> *another between the knees.*

My shrink says I'm melodramatic.
Mother always said I had a flare.
They think it'd be easy to pluck him
out, but he hisses like a geek
and digs in his teeth when I try.

The juggling man smiles a little now,
revealing those chiseled white points,
and he adds an extra spin to knife #3.
She looks away and tries to swallow.

He's never even dropped one.
I don't think he'd know how.
He was made with that stainless steel
shine already in hand, already falling
into the white glove of an open palm.

She lowers the curtain and arranges her blouse,
eyes fixed on the audience, who has nothing
to look on now, aside from her face.

OTHER PEOPLE'S CHILDREN

The boys in the hotel lobby saw
they had black swan arms. Why?
Because they were naughty,
because they were more cruel
than naughty, because they'd
never shake such sadness.

Their parents were an unkind king
and queen, but flush with devotion
for their offspring. Come darlings,
their highnesses said, there is a pet
swan in the lobby, and if we ping
her with quarters, you will see how
a pacing bird with clipped feathers
remembers her old feral rage.
See her rear up from the water
to bellow and beat her wings.

So the boys, by virtue of losing
all but the meanest sort of wonder
from their eyes, grew swan arms
and flew through the skylight faraway
into the city. Beneath them the glass
fell sharp and fast. It's a sad story,
and I am mean for telling it.
They were, after all, only children.

CURIOUS

Before he became swan or bull
or fish or flesh, the old man
became curious. It was almost pitiable
how he whispered in every ear:
What's it like, to be only here
and never there, to be one thing
and not everything, alive,
instead of everlasting?

It's not so different than you'd think –
a clock tower on a hill at dawn,
its face glowing like a separate sun.
Mist smoking up from the river
as rain falls on the bridge, a hundred
statues of martyred saints and fallen
kings. We call ourselves dust,
but you can see we don't mean it.
At the market they sell tourists streusel
and photos of a local boy eating streusel
on the stoop of an identical market –
a familiar pleasure, no doubt, collecting
postcards in shoeboxes that smell
like basements stacked high
with boxes in a basement
where splintered windows lean
on tarnished hinges. Dry leaves
pile up against the dust-coated view
of green grass and a dog sleeping
belly-faced to the sun, exhausted
from chasing his own tail,
but satisfied not to have caught it.

II.

THE FAWN

Because he'd broken out of the body, but still
had a body, the bones were making
a kind of antlered arrangement out of it.
The skeletal remains of this child,
sometimes called the deer child, are troubling
because I have an idea in mind for deer
that this boy and his pain do not fit inside.
Which is one reason to stare – to force the idea
into some other shape and then feel it fail.

What I mean is that I picked up this book
on deformities and it seemed an acceptable
thing to do because they were ancient
carvings of conjoined twins on the cathedral,
wax models of a woman with a sort of tail
growing from her forehead, photographs
of a yellowed skeleton from the seventeenth century.
The boy curiosity could not rise
from a squatting position for two years
before his death, his hydrocephelitic skull,
the caption says, has opened like a flower,
and this opening no doubt killed him.

A fawn lost half its face in our woods
and three times I have tried to bring home
the jawbone but dropped it in horror, too much
like a dead live thing to hold in my live live fingers.
As long as I didn't touch it, I could believe
dead and living are arbitrary distinctions.

An image of the body was onscreen again,
only now the doctor is pointing
at three new white streaks. Just a resident

and so unsure, he says out loud to himself,
That's not a heartbeat. That's just bone.
He doesn't want to tell me. Between the time
I saw the heartbeat and now, the baby grew
three ribs and I felt strangely proud,
as if he'd just been given a blue ribbon
at the science fair or called a polite young man
by an old woman on the bus.

In school, the same school that displayed jars
of pickled fetuses from the early days of science,
Sister Leonida showed a documentary
about the Elephant Man. He taught himself
to read using the Bible and screamed
"I am not an animal!" which was why
it was so hard, at times, to look at him.

That classroom also had a skeleton hanging
in a back closet. Hearing it was not made
of plastic, I jumped my finger off the shoulder
like you would an open sore, and squealed.
Sister Leonida was irritated to explain
most skeletons in science classrooms
come from turn-of-the-century India.
How small the bones were, how long
he must have been hungry. Untouchables
often had no choice but to sell the bodies
of their parents and children. Could I imagine
how they might have pushed tears away
with the back of their hands
as a white man handed them money?

The body is not the person, but it so clearly is.
Staring at this boy relic, I want to feel
the calcified echo of his living pain,

but the mind can never hold still.
The irregular heartbeats of thinking: *He lived,*
he lived. And then I must think it again,
because he keeps turning back into a photograph
of honeysuckled bones. *There was a time he lived.*

GREAT-AUNT MARIE DIED

In her dark box she dreamed her life
over and over again. While we all kneeled
before the splintered wood, she was
turning four and the beach was covered
with shells and desiccated starfish.
Her mother shouted, *Don't forget*
to throw the live ones back.
It would be seventy dream years
until she remembered gluing seashells
with me, until she'd hold a pink conch
cavern to my ear so I would know
how the spirits call across the waves.
I colored pictures in the pew while
my father prayed. Waiting to be born
back into my aunt's long dream,
I was an abalone ghost, nothing
but an echo humming from the deep
hollows of a shell in her hand.

THE VISIBLE SPECTRUM

Gray is the sky, gray the hawthorn tree,
gray is the moldering of the vole,

the shrike's face deep in stiffening prey.
Gray was the forest, and gray the sun.

It's hard to hold it together when it rains
so hard the magnolia blossoms fall

like flayed meat and the phone rings
someone dear trying to rasp a few last words.

When there's nothing to say.
A static of breathing, gray as the winter.

And it never passed. On a blue morning
the birds sing their rotten feeding.

YOU ARE AFRAID OF THE DARK

You are afraid of the dark,
for which you blame the raccoons,
or more to the point, your father,
who took you and your mother
into the night with a flashlight
and shotgun, then left
with both, while you held
her shaking hand. You
would follow your father
to the end of the world,
those distant birch woods
where raccoons rustle
and flash their green eyes.
His gun was firing
into the persimmon trees
and the rain of leaves and ripe fruit
fell farther and farther,
until only the crackle
of his shots and the distant baying
of the hounds could be heard.
The raccoons came then
to hiss all around:
he left you, he left you,
and now you are ours.

WANT

I came too from the wine-dark sea,
walked naked on the black-ash sand.
Who can say how I came to be here
where the child-curious wind bruises
my fruit-peeled skin? From the thistle-
scrub shade I watched myself walk out
of the ship-wreck sea. And I was
the wine-dark woman walking out
of the sea. I had always wanted to be
a bruised-fruit woman coming to land,
and I was she. Body-locked,

I could not remember my far-off shape,
only knew, standing on the black-ash
sand, that I could see a woman walking
out of the water, wanted to be a woman
walking out of the water, did not want
to be anymore a pigeon-wrung dove-slut
drying in the sun like a thistle-scrub shade,
did not want to hang by my neck over
the gore-slick grass swaying in the child-
curious wind. I did not want to be anymore
a fruit rotting over suitors' graves.

LUNARIA

Also called moonwart
because the seed pods
are frail and white like
paper moons. Also called

       money plant because
       the dry blooms look
       like coins hanging from
       a tiny tree. It grows wild

near the rotted porch
where a woman comes
to sit and watch leaves
blow through the lunaria

       all along the ghost of a blue
       house her mother had kept
       clean of drifter wildflowers
       also called weeds. A woman

whose mother's garden
has succumbed to the rustle
of brittle moons
has the look of a child

       lost at the fair such a long
       time she falls asleep on a bench
       under her jacket, which is how
       she wakes up on the porch

in the lot of lunaria scolding
with dried paper voices,
It's January! Zip up your coat
before you catch cold.

THE ABANDONED HOUSE

Luck is a mean-hoofed beast,
likes to catch you by surprise.
The lonely girl in the manor began making wishes,
which is how Luck was called down
from the forests of the mountains and into
the geometry of her estate.
He crept to her keyhole and hung
on every whispered word.

If Luck comes to your house,
you must be so careful
never to say the name of what you love,
or he will think you've grown attached.
You must never call, even in sleep,
for a quilt or curtain or sagging cellar beam,
or he'll make certain nothing is left
to name but shingles
and tar buried in the weeds.

I once kneeled at the door
when he was at the other side.
Any lonely girl can tell you
how his eye in the keyhole grows
darker and deeper until it becomes
a thorn in your brain begging Blink!

And then you blink it all: keyhole,
key, brass knob, weathervane,
chiffon skirt, combs of mother-of-pearl,
mother, father, spotless pane of glass,
bluebells in the grass.

The key in your pocket will rattle sirens
as he skips you down
the cracked concrete road.

It's exactly what you wanted.
You'll think yourself unfettered,
but Luck has driven one nail
into the sole of your shoe,
hooked the other end of his string
to the broken teeth of the attic window.
He'll never let go.

Did you think they'd take you back?
Luck will want to know.
Did you think they even could?

IN PRAISE OF ATTACHMENT

Things to win off the devil include: his charm, his sass, his perfect tan, his fiddling hands, his silver tongue, his tricky cards, his straight face, the thorn in his thumb that never lets him forget, his guppy floating sideways in the bowl with one eye up and one eye down, his tricycle, his bicycle, his crackerjack ring, his Barbie, his prom dress, his ballerina on point atop the number sixteen, his passionate crush on a boy who doesn't know he exists, his string-tied packet of letters from an ex, his twelve-pack, his six-pack, his hash and his pipe, his lighter, his match, his firebrand eye, his precious things, his cherished things, anything you ever desired, anything that ever turned your head. He'll put it all in for the chance to cleave your soul – and by yours I mean mine, and by soul I mean you're not even sure you have one to lose, but when he tells you it's a bet worth making, that's the god's honest truth, because knowing what you had when it's gone is cold comfort, but comfort nonetheless.

JUAN VALVERDE DE AMASCO

He is the anatomist most mocked by the experts
for drawing a vagina that looks like an inverted penis.

It is the perfect example, they say, of cultural
conviction triumphing over direct observation.

But I look at these drawings and think,
here's a man who believed in love above all else.

We're lost for each other and this
is how the body should be.

Of course nothing fits together that easily.

In Sex. Ed. our teacher drew on the blackboard
a face-shaped uterus with fallopian tubes

and ovaries sprouting from it like feelers.
She named the creature Peter the Bug.

We were allowed to ask anonymous questions
and she felt free to speculate.

A guy who drank enough fruit juice
probably would have punchy semen.

Because Catholicism is a religion of mysteries,
she was a paraplegic nun who pushed on a joystick
to move her wheelchair up and down the aisles.

The hallways of the convent were lined
with her paintings of roses in bloom.

When the anonymous question was asked,
she told us she had once been able to walk.
The homecoming king begged her to marry him.

Why did she become a nun? I simply loved God more,
she said but wasn't ashamed to admit

that once sitting in a pew behind a mother,
a father and their three children, I couldn't stop crying.
I thought a lot then about leaving the order,

but everyone lives with regrets – you're wrong
if you think losing your virginities will spare you that fate.

THE RENAISSANCE

Vivitur ingenio, caetera mortis errant.
-Andreas Vesalius, 1514-1564

Horror aside, I appreciate your candor.
Who could believe in the textbook's
neon liver, its hot pink lung?
But your sketch of the hanged man,
limp in his noose, holding his own
meticulously labeled organs as they
spill from his gut like flowers
dissecting themselves to death – I can relate.
And no one would deny the accuracy
of an athletic young soldier gripping
with numbered tendons the dagger
he has used to flay himself, how he stares
into the sheet of his old face.
There was a man once, who said he couldn't
bear to love me. I was just one more attachment
to grief. He tried to meditate on my decay,
to visualize the worms who would carry
my skin off one ripening mouthful
at a time. He said it was the only way
to see through the brain's vice grip.
Is it natural to be so afraid? I wonder,
Andreas, what became of you. Dead
of shipwreck in 1564, but did they find
your body? Did they even try? Are you
the curious skeleton holding another man's
skull in your bare-knuckled hand? When
you said that genius lives on, could you
already feel that alpine wind creaking
through the timber of your spine?

THE SECRETS OF FATIMA

My grandmother is a hard woman to love.
She calls my mother a Judas
then cries when we leave so nothing
can be held against her. She was blessed
by the Virgin, so she has to live,
but she does not have to let my mother
roll her wheelchair into the sun.
She does not have to try.

In Portugal, the Virgin appeared
to three children. It was 1917, the Great War
was raging. The children were hungry
that year she came to them in a cave.
My grandmother kept these clippings
wrapped in wax paper under her bed
where my mother and I found them as we
packed up and sold her house against her will.

The villagers did not believe the children
until they went to the mountains
shrouded in mist and saw the sun leaping
"a macabre dance in the sky." Two years later
two of the children were dead and it was left
to the third to write down the secrets of Fatima.

When she fell, my grandfather couldn't lift her,
so he lay by her side all night,
then called my mother in the morning.
He hoped it wasn't too early.

There were three prophesies:
The next war would begin under a banner

of celestial lights. Russia would be consecrated.
A man in white surrounded by throngs
would be shot on a hill.

When the pope was shot and lived,
he went to Russia to give blessing,
to Fatima to give thanks. He left the bullet
cut from his side at the altar. The children
would be saints, Fatima a shrine,
where my grandmother would go on the only
trip of her life. She walked the hill and prayed
to survive the operation. My grandfather
tied pads to his knees and prayed
at her side over sins he wouldn't want me to say.

The miracle of Fatima is nothing
but cryptic mumbo jumbo. When we visit
my grandmother lies in bed with her face
to the wall. We sit in the dark and I tell her
about the blue bridesmaids' dresses as my ring
makes a prism across her cheek. She wants
to know why I will not leave her in peace.

Outside, valerium turns brown in the yellow grass
and I think of my mother, a girl once
in leather shoes, kicking leaves and feeling as sad
as she's always been. When I was young
she could tell me – I wouldn't understand.
But I knew. I knew about the leaves,
and she didn't have to say, but I knew too
about the smell on the air as the wind
strips through those fragile, breaking twigs.

Now it is my job to take the girl
who swallowed a box of pink pills to the hospital

and hold her down as the nurse threads
liquid charcoal into her throat. It may or may not
be my job to dial her mother at 2 a.m. because this
is all the girl asks for when she has finished
the vomiting. Mom is high too, and they cry
across the line that they don't want to do this anymore.

Charlie, who works the night shift, likes to say
it doesn't matter if Mom put a nail up a kid's nose,
if you let him, that kid would drown himself
swimming across the river home.

It must be a terrible burden to know
however you touched your baby when she screamed,
that thread will needle up for eighty years and more.

Before he went to Fatima, the Pope went to a prison
to hear the confession of his thwarted assassin.
My grandmother saved the picture from *Time*.
The man in white places his trembling palm on the head
of a frail man trembling on his knees. A slant of light
shines through the barred window onto the intersection
of papal hand and sinner's hair. My mother unfolds
the clipping for me to see. She says this is the Calling,
the Mystery of Forgiveness. She says even if I don't
believe in miracles, I must believe in this.

REAL AS THE PANDA

My mother was already alive when the panda turned real.
It was 1950. They caught that Chinese fairy tale in a net
and brought it to the San Francisco zoo where children like
her couldn't help but ask, *Will they find the dragon too?*

And today a scientist on the radio reports that there are lakes
and rivers in the ocean, currents of pale blue running their own
ecosystems through the dark fathoms. She says, of course,
there are sensible explanations for everything, but this is so much

like a miracle to see, you must remind yourself it's all minerals
and water. Also, they say, there is the grizzly: never a body found
dead in the wild of natural causes. Gunshots and car accidents, sure,
but the grizzly who has crawled into the primeval deep to die –

only the strings of sinew are found, which are easily mistaken
for spider webs lying in a heap of dew. Things can turn
so real, maybe even this is true: the ribbons of the body
that tie a vagabond's soul across heaven and earth are cut

beginning with the headstring. But nothing solid is dead.
My mother's cheek is not cold or stiff or sagging. That was
just a dream from the bottom of the ocean, where fish glow
like lightning bugs, and even this has a scientific explanation.

My mother knew the name of every miracle. Creatures that
live in the dark are sometimes filled with bio-luminescence,
she said, as she dismembered a firefly and molded the corpse
into a ring for my finger that would glow for whole minutes.

OLM

The olm, akin to the salamander,
can be found deep in Eastern
European caves. The olm, akin
to the salamander, is pale pink
and just long enough to curl
around your wrist one time.

Once an olm was mistaken for
a baby dragon. Once an olm was
put in a jar of water in a cold
cellar and left there for 100 years.

An olm can survive in a cold
cellar for at least 100 years.

The olm, akin to the salamander,
is blind, like so many cave
dwellers. If it could see, it would
see by the light of the albino
crayfish who would see by
the light of the pale pink olm,

which we see by the light of our
fire's red sparks and orange glow
that send the olm, slick as its kin
the salamanders, slipping under
the waters of the cave creek,
a slipping so smooth and small
it sounds like nothing more than
one wet drop from a stone.

And the flapping of the olm's
stumpy arms and feet make ripples
that brush the cold lime shore,
ripples that stretch like one more
wet drop falling deep in slow
pursuit of the olm.

THE EDGE OF REASON

The narwhal: Arctic whale with a long narrow tusk extending from its muzzle. Think, if a fish were a unicorn.

Correction: Not a tusk, but a double-helixed tooth protruding through the upper left jaw into the forehead and out for open water.

Hypothesized evolutionary advantage: Offense and defense. Hypothesized evolutionary advantage: Lick your finger and hold it into the wind, thrust your tusk into the passing current. Hypothesized evolutionary advantage: Plumage, after a fashion.

Metaphysical consideration: The monoceros is a mythical horned whale monster; the monodon monoceros is a narwhal is real raises the question: Anymore can you believe anything isn't?

Bagging the narwhal is no mean feat. The first priority is to harpoon it in the brain lest it escape to die with a bellyful of arrow on some other shore. Second priority: harpoon it only after inhalation, lest in death it sink to the ocean floor.

Moral ambiguity: Given the value of their tusks, can you retrieve those filigree teeth from the poached exhales lost and littering the deep to sell on the open market?

Queen Elizabeth I held a narwhal's tusk for a scepter. One reason: When someone guts a child's sweet dream that you might have the bone to cherish, you should cherish that bone.

Question for the broken-hearted: Can you transcend these small-minded similes of pity to rejoin that great mind of being? Would it help if you could feel how gently your wet flank would brush the others and then slide away as you dipped and surfaced, surfaced and dipped, that dumb tooth you hardly think about jutted off into who knows where?

View from the port bow: A dozen dark backs undulating wavelessly through the mist. The Queen said poetically: These are the great diving beasts of a deeply held breath.

THE SOUND OF MUSIC

When I tell you I love
the song "Edelweiss"
you have to understand
that even though I too
am a sophisticate
who scorns musicals,
I was once a little girl
who stood in my grand-
father's living room
singing, *Cuckoo!*
Cuckoo! while he sipped
his scotch and laughed
at my preciosity.
And when I sing the lyrics
in your ear – *Small and*
bright, clean and white,
you look happy to meet me
– you have to understand
my grandfather only ever
had one friend, a jeweler
who also drank scotch,
and left his $10,000 Rolex
to my grandfather, who
wore it even though
it turned his wrist green,
wore it to the funeral,
where the daughter sang
in her ethereal voice. *Blossom*
of snow may you bloom
and grow, bloom and grow
forever. She couldn't take
her eyes off the casket.

You have to understand that
my grandfather kept spinning
that heavy gold around
his wrist, and when he raised
his voice to join in, he cried
to sing it. *Edelweiss, edelweiss,*
bless my homeland forever.

RAG AND BONE MAN

He walks the ornate bridges of your city,
picking up junk from the bins behind
the flea market, reciting to himself
old poems children don't read anymore.
Even you, who enjoy poetry, haven't heard these.
It's enough to make you want to follow him
to a hovel where bowls overflow with brass
doorknobs and rusty keys line the walls.
Roots of a sycamore have buckled
the foundation of his driftwood house.

He will carve that meddlesome tree into a boat.
You can come, but he will be the captain
and steer the trunk through the foaming surf.
It's a dangerous proposition. His eyes have
faded to the whites and the coin collection
alone would drag his vessel to the bottom
of the sea where pale faces hoard last
desperate breaths. Still, you must never
abandon a ruined thing. Take this dull knife –

Say it's the one your grandfather used
to cut the twine from winter hay, the knife that fell
to the dirt and the rain, the one you thought
you'd never see again. But here it is,
and all you ever lost is resurrected from rust.

ACKNOWLEDGEMENTS

Many thanks to the friends, family, teachers, and colleagues whose suggestions and support made this book possible: Jaswinder Bolina, Mary Chambers, Grace Danborn, Mark Halliday, Laura Hanneke, Christopher Howell, Jane Ellen Ibur, Jonathan Johnson, M. Patricia and Ken Nuernberger, J. Allyn Rosser, Nance Van Winckel and Maya Jewell Zeller.

Thanks also to the journals who first published these poems, sometimes in earlier forms:
"Ichthyphobia" / *Cream City Review*
"U.S. EPA Reg. No. 524-474" / *The Literary Review*
"In the Vegetable Garden" / *Poet Lore*
"Translations" / *Redactions*
"Prima Donna in Her Heaven" / *The Literary Review*
"For Emily, Who Came Sometimes to Watch the Rain" / *Conduit*
"Still Life" / *Nimrod*
"The Strange Girl Asks Politely to be Called Princess" / *Burnside Review* and *Versedaily.com*
"Paul Klee's Puppet Theater: Mr. Death and Electrical Spook" / *Bat City Review*
"A Nice Girl" / *Willow Springs*
"Other People's Children" / *Mid-American Review*
"The Fawn"/ *Lake Effect*
"Great Aunt Marie Died" / *Smartish Pace*
"The Visible Spectrum" / *The Literary Review*
"You Are Afraid of the Dark" / *Poet Lore*
"Want" / *RHINO*
"In Praise of Attachment" / *Southern Humanities Review*
"Juan Valverde de Amasco" / *Barrelhouse*
"Real as the Panda" / *Florida Review*
"Olm" / *Bateau*
"The Edge of Reason" / *Artful Dodge*
"The Sound of Music" / *Cold Mountain Review*
"Rag and Bone Man" / *Redactions*

Poetry Titles from Elixir Press

Circassian Girl by Michelle Mitchell-Foust

Imago Mundi by Michelle Mitchell-Foust

Distance From Birth by Tracy Philpot

Original White Animals by Tracy Philpot

Flow Blue by Sarah Kennedy

A Witch's Dictionary by Sarah Kennedy

Monster Zero by Jay Snodgrass

Drag by Duriel E. Harris

Running the Voodoo Down by Jim McGarrah

Assignation at Vanishing Point by Jane Satterfield

The Jewish Fake Book by Sima Rabinowitz

Recital by Samn Stockwell

Murder Ballads by Jake Adam York

Floating Girl (Angel of War) by Robert Randolph

Puritan Spectacle by Robert Strong

Keeping the Tigers Behind Us by Glenn J. Freeman

Bonneville by Jenny Mueller

Cities of Flesh and the Dead by Diann Blakely

The Halo Rule by Teresa Leo

Perpetual Care by Katie Cappello

The Raindrop's Gospel: The Trials of St. Jerome and St. Paula by Maurya Simon

Prelude to Air from Water by Sandy Florian

Let Me Open You A Swan by Deborah Bogen

Spit by Esther Lee

Rag & Bone by Kathryn Nuernberger

Fiction titles

How Things Break by Kerala Goodkin
Nine Ten Again by Phil Condon
Memory Sickness by Phong Nguyen

Limited Edition Chapbooks

Juju by Judy Moffat
Grass by Sean Aden Lovelace
X-testaments by Karen Zealand
Rapture by Sarah Kennedy
Green Ink Wings by Sherre Myers
Orange Reminds You Of Listening
by Kristin Abraham
In What I Have Done & What I Have Failed To Do by Joseph
P. Wood
Hymn of Ash by George Looney
Bray by Paul Gibbons